Power to PROSPER

BY PASTOR JOHN HAGEE & PASTOR MATT HAGEE

HageeMinistries

ISBN 1-56908-037-2

CONTENTS

chapter
one

Jesus Christ gave us thirty-eight parables. Sixteen of those thirty-eight parables deal with money management. Do you realize that more is said in the New Testament about money than heaven and hell combined?

Five times more is said about money than prayer. There are five hundred verses on both prayer and faith, yet there are over two thousand verses dealing with money and possessions. The fact is that you will either master your money, or your money will master you.

Who wouldn't want God to explode their prosperity? Who wouldn't like the windows of heaven to open and for God to bless them with blessings they could not contain?

Deuteronomy 8:18
"And you shall remember
the LORD your God, for *it is* He
who gives you power to get wealth."

PRINCIPLE 1

You will never prosper until you believe and confess that it is God's will for you to prosper!

If God blessed Abraham with lavish prosperity, He can pour blessings of prosperity upon you that you will be unable to contain. You must confess His Word for your prosperity!

"Beloved, I pray that you may prosper in all things and be in health, just as your soul prospers." (3 John 1:2)

"Both riches and honor *come* from You, And You reign over all..." (1 Chronicles 29:12)

"Blessed *is* the man who walks not in the counsel of the ungodly, nor stands in the path of sinners, nor sits in the seat of the scornful; But his delight *is* in the law of the LORD, and in His law he meditates day and night. He shall be like a tree planted by the rivers of water, that brings forth its fruit in its season, whose leaf also shall not wither; and whatever he does shall prosper." (Psalm 1:1-3)

PRINCIPLE 2

God owns all the wealth in the world!

"For *the kingdom of heaven is* as a man traveling to a far country, *who* called his own servants and delivered his goods to them." (Matthew 25:14)

There are two revolutionary implications in this verse: First, it is God's money and He has the right to whatever He wants. As the Owner He has rights; as the steward I have responsibilities. Second, since all my money is God's money, every spending decision I make is a spiritual decision. Your checkbook is a spiritual reflection of your love for Christ.

You are a steward, while God is the Owner. You will give an account to God for how you managed His resources.

PRINCIPLE 3

All of God's wealth belongs to His children!

You do not qualify for God's abundance until you become God's child. You cannot pray "Our Father which art in heaven" until you receive Jesus.

The Bible says in John 14:6, "No one comes to the Father except through Me."

There are two families in the Bible: The family of God ("Our Father in heaven") and the family of Satan (Jesus said in John 8:44, "You are of *your* father the devil"). When God is your father, all His wealth belongs to you. He has promised to take care of His children. So with the question: Why are people in India starving? The answer is: God is not their father. Their God is a cow or rat.

"Therefore let no one boast in men. For all things are yours... and you *are* Christ's, and Christ *is* God's." (1 Corinthians 3:21-23)

Romans 8:17 declares, "And if children, then heirs - heirs of God and joint heirs with Christ." Not equal heirs (half and half), but joint heirs. All that He has is yours, and all that you have is His.

At Calvary, I brought Him my poverty, and He brought the riches of Abraham. When Jesus was on the Cross, He was hungry, thirsty, and naked. When He died, He was buried in a borrowed tomb, but when He cried, "It is finished!" poverty died. I was a Gentile, and He adopted me and made me a child of the King. I now have the royal Blood of heaven flowing in my veins. I am saved, sealed, and sanctified.

PRINCIPLE 4

The difference between living a life of prosperity and a life of poverty is a matter of choice!

Deuteronomy 30:19 says, "...I have set before you life and death, blessing and cursing; therefore choose life." Blessing is a result of choice.

Luke 6:38 says, "Give, and it will be given to you: good measure, pressed down, shaken together, and running over." The fact is that givers gain, but you have to make the choice to be a giver. If you are not receiving it, it's because you are not giving it. The Word says to "give, and it will be given to you." Should you expect to gain when you give? Yes!

Tithing is a choice. If you choose to not tithe, you will be living under a financial curse. What is your choice? Would you rather be blessed by Almighty God or live under a curse?

Diligence is also a choice. Proverbs 13:4 says, "The soul of a lazy man desires, and has nothing; But the soul of the diligent shall be made rich." What does this mean? Go to work! The only place you find success before work is in the dictionary. God provides worms for birds, but He doesn't shove them down their throats. Fight poverty the American way... get a job! Your financial prosperity tomorrow will be determined by your obedience today. It is your choice!

God's children have historically been prosperous. In Genesis 13, Abraham is described as having many cattle along with silver and gold. This description is not of being spiritually rich, but of being "literally" rich.

Solomon was wealthy. Archaeologists have discovered that Solomon had hinges on his horse stables that were gold plated. King David said, "The Lord is my shepherd, I shall not want." That was a confession of prosperity. David gave one hundred million for the building of the temple. That is not too bad for someone who started out with five rocks and a slingshot.

The doctrine of Popini in the Middle Ages stated, "Poverty is spiritual." That is not so! Poverty is a curse that is a result of sin. Sin produces poverty. One drunk driver can instantly change the lives of a carload of healthy, happy people. Sexual sin brings poverty, drug addiction brings poverty, alcoholism brings poverty, and crime brings poverty. There is a high price for low living... the wages of sin is death.

PRINCIPLE 5

Jesus proclaimed His personal wealth!

If wealth were a negative thing, why would God the Father give it to His Son, Jesus Christ? Revelation 5:12, "Worthy is the Lamb who was slain to receive power, and riches, and wisdom, and strength, and honor, and glory and blessing!" These seven blessings are given to the Son and to the Church.

Matthew 13:44 says, "The kingdom of heaven is like treasure hidden in a field..." Treasure excites people. John the Revelator described his eternal home as having foundations of twelve kinds of precious stones, twelve gates of solid pearl, and streets made of gold.

Mansions have been designed by the Architect of the Ages for God's children.

People like to say that Jesus was poor. When was He poor? Jesus was poor while He was on the Cross. Why was He poor on the Cross? He was poor because He took the poverty of those who accepted Him and replaced it with the wealth of Abraham.

PRINCIPLE 6

God wants you to invest in yourself!

"Lay up for yourself treasures in heaven." The day is going to come when all you will have is what you have given to God. There are two words that Christians tend to confuse: self-interest (which is good) and selfishness (which is a spiritual cancer).

It is in my self-interest to be saved. The options are heaven and hell. It is in my self-interest to be happy. The Bible says, "A merry heart does good, like medicine" and "The joy of the Lord is your strength." It is in your self-interest to invest in the Kingdom of God because God controls the economy on both sides of the Jordan River.

Matthew 19:29 says, "And everyone who has left houses or brothers or sisters or father or mother or wife or children or lands, for My name's sake, shall receive a hundredfold, and inherit eternal life." What is the rate of return on one hundredfold? One hundredfold has a return of ten thousand percent. The Kingdom of God pays ten thousand percent, so it is in your self-interest to invest all you can get your hands on.

PRINCIPLE 7

Jesus taught us to invest wisely by investing in things that are permanent!

Jesus taught us that it is not in our self-interests to invest in something that moths can eat, rust can decay, or that thieves can carry off. Dewdrops are as pretty as diamonds until the sun comes out because they are not permanent. The Bible teaches us that the world shall pass away. Simply said, the earth is not permanent.

"But the day of the Lord will come as a thief in the night, in which the heavens will pass away with a great noise, and the elements will melt with a fervent heat; both the earth and the works that are in it will be burned up." (2 Peter 3:10)

You need to invest wisely in the Kingdom of God. Lay up treasures for yourselves and invest in the Gospel!

PRINCIPLE 8

Why give? God has created a universe where it is impossible to receive without giving!

The fact is that everything that God controls gives. If something within you resents giving, that something is not of God. Giving is the only proof you have that greed has not become cancer on your soul.

The sun gives light without which the world would cease. The plants provide food, and the clouds give rain. God the Father so loved the world that He gave His only begotten Son. Givers gain. You do not qualify to receive from God or anyone else until you give.

The Bible commands, "Give and it will be given to you." Until you give, you will not qualify to receive the power to get wealth.

PRINCIPLE 9

God Almighty controls the economy of America... and God controls your income!

Your source is God, not the United States' government. The Bible says, "It is He who gives you power to get wealth." When you give to God, He controls your income. There is no such thing as a fixed income in the Kingdom of God. Your income is controlled by your giving.

A widow in the Old Testament gave her last piece of bread to Elijah. After that, she and her son prepared to die of starvation. This was a time of great depression. She was a single parent, and Elijah had asked for her last slice of bread. She gave it to him. As soon as she gave what was in her hand, God supernaturally caused the jar of flour not to be used up or the jug of oil to run dry. At that point, she had more than she could use. She had supernatural abundance, and that is what God wants for you.

How do you get it? When you let go of what is in your hands towards God, then God will let go of what is in His hands towards you. The decision to live in poverty or prosperity is yours. Your future financial condition will be determined by your obedience. God is not limited to what you have. He is limited by what you give.

PRINCIPLE 10

There are two kinds of givers: reason givers and revelation givers!

Reason givers are controlled by their minds. They do not ask God how much they should give; they ask their CPA.

Revelation givers are controlled by the Holy Spirit. They see God as their Supplier. Revelation givers do not give according to what they have, but according to what God can supply. Revelation givers know that the earth is going to pass away and they understand the true value of a soul.

It is important to remember that as soon as you do something special for God, there is always someone saying that you did wrong. Matthew 26 tells the story of Mary. She broke an alabaster box with twelve ounces of precious oil over the head and body of Jesus as a memorial of her love. Judas yelled out that she had wasted a year's wages on it and that the money could have been used to feed and clothe the poor. Jesus said that wherever the Gospel was preached in the whole world "what this woman has done will be a memorial to her."

Remember, it is the Lord who gives you the power to get wealth. Give, and it shall be given unto you. God has given you His very best, will you give Him yours?

Chapter two

Everything God does on earth comes from the principle of seedtime and harvest. Genesis 8:22 states, "While the earth remains, seedtime and harvest, cold and heat, winter and summer, and day and night shall not cease."

Consider the spiritual realm. How did Jesus Christ come to earth? The answer: seedtime and harvest. Genesis 3:15, "The seed of a woman shall crush the head of the serpent." The Holy Ghost planted a seed into Mary's womb, and the kingdom of Satan was defeated.

Consider the physical realm. How did you get here? The answer: seedtime and harvest. These two events were separated by nine months.

Consider the financial realm. Luke 6:38 states, "Give and it will be given to you." What is the "it" that you have planted? If you plant an apple seed, you will get apples. If you plant a peach seed, you will get peaches. If you plant finances, you will get finances. The Bible says that whatsoever a man soweth that shall he also reap.

You must be careful about what you plant. You will reap what you sow. If you sow wild oats, you will reap them.

PRINCIPLE 1

Giver's Gain!

If you give to the Lord, you should be expecting a gain! "Give, and it will be given to you: good measure, pressed down, shaken together, and running over." (Luke 6:38) Every time God gives you an opportunity to give, He is also providing you a chance to increase your income.

Some of you think that because you are so far behind financially, that you will never catch up. That is wrong. God is able to make it up to you by giving you everything you need and more, so that there will not only be enough for your needs but plenty left over to give joyfully to others. Your only hope of catching up is planting a seed in the Kingdom of God. The Kingdom of God is the only surefire investment you will ever have.

PRINCIPLE 2

You must plant your seed before you can expect an increase!

The Bible says, "there is a time to plant, and a time to pluck *what is* planted." (Eccl. 3:2) Without seedtime, it is impossible to have a harvest. If you give nothing, you get nothing. God can increase what you give one hundredfold, but nothing times nothing equals nothing.

Jesus said, "Most assuredly, I say to you, unless a grain of wheat falls into the ground and dies, it remains alone." (John 12:24) When what you have in your hand is not enough to meet your need it becomes your seed. You can do three things with a seed: eat it, feed it to your cows, or plant it. The fact is that there is no chance of increase until you plant it. You cannot have financial freedom without increase, and you cannot have increase without first planting your seed.

Many people say, "I have nothing to give." That is wrong. 2 Corinthians 9:10-11 says, "He who supplies seed to the sower, and bread for food, supply and multiply the seed you have *sown* and increase the fruits of your righteousness, while *you are* enriched in everything for all liberality, which causes thanksgiving through us to

God." You do not have to understand God's economic system for it to work. Isaiah 55:8-9, "'For My thoughts *are* not your thoughts, nor *are* your ways My ways,' says the LORD. 'For *as* the heavens are higher than the earth, so are My ways higher than your ways, and My thoughts than your thoughts.'" When you plant your seed in the Kingdom of God, the Lord will multiply it far better than Wall Street.

What causes an economic crash? Hoarding. People stop investing their money because they develop a lack of confidence. The economy then freezes up, and that is followed by a recession and crash.

In God's economic system, He gives to you so you can give to others. The money in God's system is constantly in circulation. His economy can never crash. Plant your money into the Kingdom of God. That is when you become wealthy enough to have financial freedom.

PRINCIPLE 3

A tithe is not a debt we owe; it is a seed we sow!

A tithe is ten percent of your income. Do I expect you to give ten percent of your income to God? No I don't, but He does. He controls your income.

Leviticus 27:30 says, "All the tithe of the land, *whether* of the seed of the land *or* of the fruit of the tree, *is* the LORD's." Are you giving what is right, or what is left? Malachi 3:10 says, "Bring all the tithes into the storehouse." Not some, ALL!

The fact is that you do not use your electricity and pay the water company. You give your tithes where you are spiritually fed. Why tithe? The Lord commands it. Refusal to tithe is rebellion against God. If you do not tithe, you live under a financial curse. Malachi 3:9 states, "You are cursed with a curse, for you have robbed Me."

Prosperity is a decision. You tithe because God promises to bless you when you do.

"'And try Me now in this,' says the LORD of hosts. 'If I will not open for you the windows of heaven and pour out for you *such* blessing that *there will* not *be room* enough *to receive it*.'" (Malachi 3:10)

PRINCIPLE 4

You determine the size of your harvest when you sow your seed!

Do you need a big harvest? Sow a lot of seed. 2 Corinthians 9:6, "He who sows sparingly will also reap sparingly, and he who sows bountifully will also reap bountifully."

"For with the same measure that you use, it will be measured back to you." (Luke 6:38)

Everyone agrees that prosperity is better than poverty. What most people don't realize is that it is your choice. You determine the size of your harvest when the offering plate comes by. Plant your seed according to your need. Attack your lack with seedtime and harvest.

Your prosperity gives God pleasure. "Let the LORD be magnified, Who has pleasure in the prosperity of His servant." (Psalm 35:27) The Bible also says that God wishes above all things that you prosper and be in good health. God rejoices when His children receive wealth. If you are not prospering, it is not God's fault. If you are not receiving, then you are not giving.

PRINCIPLE 5

Plant your seed in good ground!

What is good ground? Good ground is the Kingdom of God. Jesus said, "Seek first the Kingdom of God and His righteousness, and all these things shall be added to you."

The fact is that not every church is good ground. Not every television ministry is good ground. Why? Many churches and ministries do not represent the true Kingdom of God.

A church that ordains homosexuals into the ministry, denies the virgin birth, or contradicts the inspired Word of God does not represent the true Kingdom of God. Any church or ministry that supports abortion does not represent the true Kingdom of God. The Bible says that abortion is death. Any television ministry that promotes positive thinking over repentance and confession to Jesus Christ our Lord and Savior is preaching false doctrine and therefore does not represent the true Kingdom of God.

CHAPTER TWO

PRINCIPLE 6

Be patient! You must wait for the harvest!

"Do not become sluggish, but imitate those who through faith and patience inherit the promises." (Hebrews 6:12)

"But the ones *that* fell on the good ground are those who, having heard the word with a noble and good heart, keep *it* and bear fruit with patience." (Luke 8:15)

Many of you plant your seed abundantly in good ground but kill your harvest, because you are impatient.

"But if we hope for what we do not see, we eagerly wait for *it* with perseverance." (Romans 8:25)

"For you have need of endurance, so that after you have done the will of God, you may receive the promise." (Hebrews 10:36)

"Let us not grow weary while doing good, for in due season we shall reap if we do not lose heart." (Galatians 6:9)

Esau sold his birthright for a bowl of potage because of impatience. His impatience killed his harvest. If you invest one thousand dollars in the Kingdom of God through your church offering, do not look for the one hundredfold return before you leave that morning. Impatience will kill your harvest.

You can also kill your harvest by murmuring. Mark 11:23 says, "For assuredly, I say to you, whoever says to this mountain, 'Be removed and cast into the sea' and does not doubt in his heart, but believes that those things he says will be done, he will have whatever he says."

Murmuring sounds like this: "God's not going to come through this time; I've waited long enough; Where is God when you really need Him?" Murmuring will cause God to cancel your harvest. When Israel murmured against God, He sent snakes to bite them. The snake is the symbol of Satan. When you murmur, you are inviting snakes to enter your life. You are inviting Satan and his demon power to destroy your harvest.

PRINCIPLE 7

The decision to live in poverty or prosperity is yours!

"I call heaven and earth as witnesses today against you, *that* I have set before you life and death, blessing and cursing; therefore choose life, that both you and your descendants may live." (Deuteronomy 30:19)

Obedience is the equal of prosperity, while disobedience results in a curse. Which do you choose?

PRINCIPLE 8

God is trying to establish His Kingdom on earth!

We talk mostly about God getting us into heaven, but the Bible teaches us that God is trying to establish His Kingdom on earth. The Lord's Prayer states, "Your Kingdom come. Your will be done on earth as *it is* in heaven." (Matthew 6:10) God sought to establish His Kingdom in the Garden of Eden, but Adam and Eve disobeyed. They went from abundance to lack. God then sought to dwell with man in the Tabernacle in the wilderness. God lived in the Holy of Holies, and there was not one sick or feeble among them. God's presence filled Solomon's temple until men could not stand in the presence of God.

"I, John, saw the holy city, New Jerusalem coming down out of heaven from God... and I heard a loud voice from heaven saying, 'Behold, the tabernacle of God *is* with men, and He will dwell with them.'" (Revelations 21:2-3)

From Genesis to Revelation, God has been trying to get heaven into earth. Heaven has nothing but staggering abundance, and God wants His Kingdom principles to rule the earth. Why hasn't it? We have rejected His principle of seedtime and harvest.

PRINCIPLE 9

Hard times are wrong times to stop giving to God!

You give your way out of financial lack. In Psalm 37:25 David said, "I have been young, and *now* am old; yet I have not seen the righteous forsaken, nor His descendants begging bread."

Dr. Cho's church in Korea has eight hundred thousand members. How did they finance their building program? It started with one woman bringing her rice bowl and laying it at the altar of the church. The congregation then followed. The congregation's seed allowed such an abundant harvest that they built the church with cash.

PRINCIPLE 10

If it was sinful for you to enjoy material blessings then God would not have given them to Abraham, Isaac, Jacob, David, Solomon, or His Son, Jesus Christ!

"Worthy is the Lamb who was slain to receive power and riches and wisdom and strength and honor and glory and blessing!" (Revelation 5:12)

The prayer of Jabez found in 1 Chronicles 4:10 says, "And Jabez called on the God of Israel saying, 'Oh, that You would bless me indeed, and enlarge my territory, that Your hand would be with me, and that You would keep *me* from evil, that I may not cause pain!'" What was God's response? God granted Jabez his request.

When you turn loose of what is in your hand to God, God will turn loose of what is in His hand to you.

CHAPTER TWO

Chapter three

Money is an exciting topic. If you mention the word, it will cause people's blood pressure to rise, nostrils to flare, and sweat will roll down their foreheads.

You have been reading about Bible principles in mastering your money. Before I introduce new principles, I want to review a few.

GIVER'S GAIN

You must understand the principles of farming to understand God's principle of seedtime and harvest. Jesus said, "Behold, a sower went out to sow... (the seed) fell on good ground and yielded a crop." (Matthew 13:3-8)

YOU MUST PLANT YOUR SEED

If there is no seedtime, there can be no harvest time. If you did not send your ship out, don't look for your ship to come in.

TITHE

You must tithe because God commands it. If you do not tithe, you will live under God's economic curse. Malachi 3:9 says, "You are cursed with a curse."

YOU DETERMINE THE SIZE OF YOUR HARVEST

You determine the size of your harvest when you sow your seed. Do you need a big harvest? Sow lots of seed.

PLANT YOUR SEED IN GOOD GROUND

Not every ministry is good ground. Not every church represents the Kingdom of God. Investing in ministries whose ground is not good is like throwing seed on an asphalt parking lot.

YOU MUST BE PATIENT

You must wait for the harvest. Two things can kill your harvest: impatience and murmuring.

PRINCIPLE 1

God gives you wealth not to hoard it, but to be a blessing to other people!

We plant by reaching out to others and then reap as God reaches out to us. God said to Abraham, "I will bless you… and you shall be a blessing."

Abraham is our spiritual father. Galatians 3:29 states, "If you *are* Christ's, then you are Abraham's seed, and heirs according to the promise."

If your spiritual father is wealthy, if it is your divine assignment to be a blessing, then how can you fulfill God's commission to be a blessing without abundance? How can you feed the poor, clothe the naked, build churches or a television ministry if you cannot clothe and feed yourself?

The fact is, if you are serving a god limited in finances then you are not serving the God of Abraham, Isaac, and Jacob.

"The silver *is* Mine and the gold *is* Mine, says the LORD of hosts." (Haggai 2:8)

It is a blessing to walk up to a home where a family is

carrying out their possessions because they could not pay their rent, and pay their rent for them. How can you do that without abundance? God gives you wealth to bless other people, not so you can live like King Tut, but so you can bless others. "You ask and do not receive, because you ask amiss, that you may spend *it* on your pleasures." (James 4:3)

Wealth is given to those who make evangelism a top priority. Deuteronomy 8:18 declares, "Remember the LORD your God, for *it is* He who gives you power to get wealth, that He may establish His covenant which He swore to your fathers, as *it is* this day."

PRINCIPLE 2

Change your attitude about abundance to receive abundance!

Your thoughts determine your destiny. You can live life without limit or live life on your pity pot. It is your choice.

Some people have a poverty complex. It goes like this, "Jesus was poor. I am poor. I am like Jesus." That is so wrong; Jesus wasn't poor.

Jesus had a nice house. John 1:38-39 says, "Jesus turned, and seeing them following, said to them, 'What do you seek?' They said to Him, 'Rabbi, where are You staying?' He said to them, 'Come and see.' They came and saw where He was staying, and remained with Him that day." The fact is that the house was big enough to hold that crowd.

Jesus wore the finest clothes. John 19:23 tells us that Jesus had a seamless robe. It was so valuable that the Roman soldiers gambled for it at Calvary. Jesus had enough money that He assigned one of His disciples to carry the money bag. That is not poor! If you are walking around with your lower lip trembling saying, "Jesus was poor; I am poor, and that makes me spiritual because I am like Jesus," you are wrong and in deception.

Wake up and smell the coffee. You don't understand the principles of seedtime and harvest. God wants to give you wells you did not dig, vineyards you didn't plant, and open the windows of heaven and pour out a blessing you cannot contain.

Some people feel guilty about having nice things. Jesus didn't; He enjoyed nice things. He does not care how many things you own as long as the things do not own you. It is not about possessions; it is about priorities. God demands to be first.

PRINCIPLE 3

God's purpose produces God's power for financial freedom!

You will not have God's power or His prosperity until you find God's purpose for your life. God has a purpose for your life. You need to find it.

"And we know that all things work together for good to those who love God, to those who are the called according to *His* purpose." (Romans 8:28)

God said to Elijah, "Go to the house of the widow woman; I will feed you there." God had an exact place for Elijah to serve. He also has an exact place for you to serve. If you find that place for you to serve, you will find His power, His provision, and a supernatural abundance.

How many of you have lived in a land of not enough or just enough? How many of you would prefer to live in the promised land of more than enough? The fact is you cannot get to the Promised Land without first leaving Egypt. You have to give up what you have to get what God wants to give you. Good is the enemy of better, and better is the enemy of best.

If you are in Egypt or the wilderness, start marching toward the Promised Land. You are Abraham's seed, and he didn't live on just enough. Break out of your wilderness complex, out of mediocrity and into magnificence. Attack your lack with seedtime and harvest. Reach for life without limit in the Promised Land.

Get a new attitude, believe for a financial breakthrough, and press toward the Land flowing with milk and honey. God wants to shower you with abundance, but He can't as long as you stay in Egypt.

PRINCIPLE 4

Release the anointing on your finances!

"It shall come to pass in that day *that* his burden will be taken away from your shoulder, and his yoke from your neck, and the yoke will be destroyed because of the anointing oil." (Isaiah 10:27)

What is the anointing? The anointing removes burdens and destroys yokes. If burdens are not removed and yokes not destroyed, there was no anointing.

PRINCIPLE 5

Release God's anointing to get out of debt!

God can supernaturally bless your finances to help you get out of debt. You will never have financial freedom if you allow yourself to be trapped in the quicksand of debt.

Debt is not a sin, but it is dangerous.

"The borrower *is* servant (slave) to the lender." (Proverbs 22:7) Many of you are slaves to banks. You must learn the most important sentence in human speech: "I cannot afford it."

There are three questions you need to ask yourself before buying anything: "Do I need this? Does my spouse agree with me about making this debt? And how am I going to pay this back?"

Debt destroys your relationship with God. You sink yourself into debt, lose your job, and get bitter at God because your home gets repossessed. The fact is that debt creates another god, the banker. If we came before God with the same humility with which we go see the banker, revival would explode in America.

Plant your seed according to your need. Break the debt bondage. You will not get out of debt overnight, but you will little by little.

PRINCIPLE 6

The final step to financial freedom is to place your seed in anointed hands!

How do you get your 'not enough' turned into 'more than enough'? John 6:9-13 tells the story of a little boy who had five barley loaves and two small fish. Jesus needed to feed 5000 people, and He turned to this young boy who gladly gave his lunch (seed). The young boy placed it into the anointed hands of Jesus, and those hands multiplied it at least fifteen thousand times. The boy then went home with twelve baskets full of leftovers.

They started with not enough, and they ended with more than enough.

When you put your seed in anointed hands, God will multiply it supernaturally beyond your wildest dreams.

Chapter four

The name "Jabez" is a synonym for pain.

His own mother said, "Because I bore him in pain." This is not the pain of childbirth, it is a greater pain not mentioned in the text.

Pain drove Jabez to seek a better life. Many of you suffer from inner pain: The pain of a bitter divorce, bankruptcy, betrayal, rejection, unexpected tragedy, or a health crisis.

Jesus Christ is a portrait of pain. Isaiah said, "He is a Man of sorrows and acquainted with grief." Jesus had the pain of being illegitimate, a homeless refugee, a hated minority, being oppressed by the government, slandered by the religious leaders, betrayed by His friends, and ultimately by death on the Cross.

The secret of living a great life is transforming tragedy into triumph. Forget what is behind you. St. Paul said (Phil. 3:13-14), "Forgetting those things which are behind and reaching forward to those things which are ahead, I press toward the goal for the prize of the upward call of God in Christ Jesus."

You must remember that life is a road, not a parking lot. Life is a battle, not a rest home. Life is a school, not a cemetery. Move on beyond your adversities and acrimony. Move forward beyond your tragedies and tears. Move past your setbacks and suffering.

Helen Keller moved beyond the pain of blindness to inspire the world with academic genius. Beethoven moved beyond the pain of deafness and wrote masterful music the world still loves to hear. Abraham Lincoln moved beyond the pain of a nervous breakdown and eleven political defeats to become one of the greatest Presidents of the United States of America.

St. Paul wrote in 2 Corinthians 4:8-9, "We *are* hard-pressed on every side, yet not crushed; *we are* perplexed, but not in despair; persecuted, but not forsaken, struck down, but not destroyed...", we are more than conquerors through Christ our Lord.

Jesus Christ moved beyond the pain of Calvary to the joyous shout of the Resurrection morning. Jesus said, "Be of good cheer, I have overcome the world."

Jabez moved beyond the unspoken pain of his youth to reach for a life without limit. He wanted a life more abundant, that was super-charged with miracle power. Jabez wanted a life by faith, not by sight. He got that life.

The pain of your past will be diminished by the promise of your future. What you have been through is not as important as what you are going to do. The past is over.

Today is the first day of the rest of your life. The Bible declares, "Weeping may endure for a night, but joy *comes* in the morning." (Psalm 30:5)

"Though your beginning was small, yet your latter end would increase abundantly." (Job 8:7)

"For I know the thoughts that I think toward you, says the LORD, thoughts of peace and not of evil, to give you a future and a hope." (Jeremiah 29:11)

"I will go before you and make the crooked places straight; I will break in pieces the gates of bronze and cut the bars of iron. I will give you the treasures of darkness and hidden riches of secret places, that you may know that I, the LORD, who call *you* by your name, *Am* the God of Israel." (Isaiah 45:2-3)

Jabez asked God to help him live life without limit!

The resurrection story is a story of life without limit. Since the Genesis of time, man has looked at death as the ultimate end, the limit. But when Jesus died, He rose from the grave and defeated death, hell, and the grave.

Because Jesus lives we shall live also. Death is not the end; it is the gateway to Glory. Death is not farewell; it is the beginning of God's tomorrow.

My body will wear out, but I will have a new body in the new Jerusalem. I will also have a new name, a new robe, a new mansion, and a thousand years from now, I will be shouting on the hills of Glory in my glorified, disease-free body. Life has no limits.

Jabez prayed: "Oh, that you would bless me indeed, and enlarge my territory." (I Chronicles 4:10)

Jabez prayed for God's blessing.

What is a blessing? A blessing is the impartation of the supernatural power of God into a human life by the spoken Word of God's delegated authority.

Words have life and power. Words spoken under the anointing shape the destiny of individuals, families, and nations. The first thing God did after creating Adam and Eve was to bless them "Then God blessed them, and God said to them, 'Be fruitful and multiply; fill the earth and subdue it [spiritual warfare]; have dominion...'" (Genesis 1:28) Take charge over your life or someone else will.

God blessed Abraham in Genesis 12:3, "I will bless those who bless you..." Jewish fathers and mothers bless their children every Friday at Sabbath. They do this because of the supernatural power of the blessing. Their children go out and live their lives without limit because their parents bless them with the blessing of Abraham.

Jacob blessed his twelve sons on his deathbed. Everything that Jacob spoke into the lives of his sons came true. The power of the blessing followed those boys until the last day of their lives. When a spiritual authority speaks the blessing over you, no person can steal or stop your blessing. Satan himself cannot stop God's blessings for you.

God's blessings and His abundance are limited only by us, not His resources, power, or willingness. God wants to give to you but cannot unless you ask for His blessing.

God's provision is in His promises!

2 Peter 1:2-3 says, "Grace and peace be multiplied to you in the knowledge of God and of Jesus our Lord, as His divine power has given to us all things that *pertain* to life..." God has already given to you all things that we need for life, but if you have not asked for it, it will sit in Heaven wasted.

God's provision is for everyone. "And God *is* able to make all grace abound toward you, that you, always having all sufficiency in all *things*, may have an abundance for every good work." (2 Corinthians 9:8)

The power of proclamation in receiving God's provision!

The prayer of Jabez is a proclamation. I encourage you to pray it each morning and evening, in faith, to live a life spiritually, emotionally, and financially without limit.

The word "proclaim" comes from the Latin meaning to "shout forth." A proclamation is spiritual warfare, and it releases God's Word into our personal battle.

"So shall My word be that goes forth from My mouth; it shall not return to Me void. But it shall accomplish what I please, and it shall prosper *in the thing* for which I sent it." (Isaiah 55:11)

In Hebrews 3:1 Jesus Christ is called, "The High Priest of our confession."

Look at the power of God's spoken Word in Genesis 1:3, "Then God said, 'Let there be light'; and there was light." God didn't think it or meditate on it, He spoke it. "By the word of the Lord the heavens were made, and all the host of them by the breath of His mouth." (Psalm 33:6)

Revelation 19 says that when Jesus returns to earth at Armageddon, out of His mouth shall come a two-edged sword with which He shall smite the nations of the world.

How is the power of God released into your life? The power of God is released through the spoken Word of

God. As powerful as God is, He cannot answer prayer until you pray. He does not answer a petition that has not been presented.

Moses took hold of the rod. It became a spiritual weapon. "Let the saints be joyful in glory; let them sing aloud on their beds. *Let* the high praises of God *be* in their mouth, and a two-edged sword in their hand, to execute vengeance on the nations, and punishments on the peoples; to bind their kings with chains, and their nobles with fetters of iron; to execute on them the written judgment - this honor have all His saints. Praise the LORD!" (Psalm 149:5-9)

Moses learned to stretch out his rod. You must learn to use your authority which is the spoken Word of God. Learn to make Scriptural proclamations. In moments of doubt or fear about the future, declare this Scriptural proclamation found in Jeremiah 29:11, "For I know the thoughts that I think toward you, says the LORD, thoughts of peace and not of evil, to give you a future and a hope."

Do you need self-defense from sickness? Make the proclamation of Psalm 118:17, "I shall not die, but live, and declare the works of the LORD." You need to say: "By His stripes I am now being healed because He is the Lord that heals all of my diseases; The angel of the Lord encamps round about me, no plague shall come near my dwelling; I confess that the Word of God is life and health to my flesh; I receive divine health now, in the name of Jesus."

The Word of God can be self-defense from attack. You can confess through the name of Jesus Christ that, "no weapon formed against me shall prosper, and every tongue that rises against me in judgment I shall condemn. This is the heritage of the servants of the LORD, and their righteousness is from Me". (Isaiah 54:17)

"The eternal God *is your* refuge, and underneath *are* the everlasting arms; He will thrust out the enemy from before you, and will say, 'Destroy!'" (Deuteronomy 33:27)

The Word of God is a proclamation in financial need. Joshua 1:8 declares, "This Book of the Law shall not depart from your mouth... for then you will make your way prosperous, and then you will have good success."

"Beloved, I pray that you may prosper in all things and be in health, just as your soul prospers." (3 John 2)

It is God's will for you to be successful and blessed in all that you do. Take authority as a Believer and proclaim His Word for your needs.

chapter
five

We live in a time when everyone needs wise financial counsel. Where can a person find sound financial advice? Not from the government! With a national debt racing past sixteen trillion, it would take more than forty-three thousand years paying one million per day just to break even. The idea that Congress will balance the budget is a pipe dream.

You seldom get sound financial advice from relatives or friends. Only two percent of Americans are financially independent at the age of sixty-five. According to the Social Security Administration, eighty-five out of every one hundred Americans have less than two hundred and fifty dollars in their savings when they reach age sixty-five.

Where can you find sound financial advice? How would you like to own the most astute financial guide ever printed? Its wisdom and power defy anything Wall Street has ever published. It is time tested, and its proven financial principles are rock solid. It will teach you how to master your money and how to release God's power and wealth into your life.

What is the guide? The Bible.

The purpose of abundance is not to hoard it but to share it.

2 Corinthians 9:8 says, "...that you, always having all sufficiency in all *things*, may have an abundance for every good work." Never in the New Testament is it written, "If we have enough money, we'll do it." Their plans didn't depend on money. They found the will of God. God provided for every good work.

One specific good work is to provide a dwelling place for God on Earth.

We often talk as if the ultimate goal is to get to Heaven, but it's clear in Scripture that the ultimate goal is to get Heaven to earth. In the final chapters of Revelation, God brings Heaven down to earth. "Then I, John, saw the holy city, New Jerusalem, coming down out of Heaven from God, prepared as a bride adorned for her husband." (Revelation 21:2)

The fact is that from the creation in Genesis to the closing scenes of Revelation, it is God's objective to dwell with man. Look at the tabernacle. God provided in advance all the gold and silver necessary to build the tabernacle. The tabernacle would cost in excess of one hundred million dollars in today's currency. Every piece of furniture, fabric, gold, silver, and brass was designed with exact detail. It was of the highest quality.

In Genesis 15:13-14, God said to Abraham, "Know certainly that your descendants will be strangers in a land *that is* not theirs, and will serve them, and they will afflict them four hundred years. And also the nation whom they serve I will judge; afterward, they shall come out with great possessions."

Was it just for the Israelites to plunder the Egyptians? Yes. God had been keeping records for four hundred years; Jews worked as slaves. They collected their wages that day plus interest. God will not allow the Devil to steal your wages.

God gave them wealth for a purpose: to build the tabernacle. He wanted to live there in the Holy of Holies.

Exodus 35:4-5 tells us, "And Moses spoke... whoever *is* of a willing heart, let him bring it as an offering to the LORD." In the Old Testament, tithes were never used to build churches. Churches were built with freewill offerings. The tithe was demanded. The point here is that if you take God's money (tithe) and build God's house, what have you given to God? Nothing.

What was the result of Moses' freewill offering? Exodus 36:5-7 tells us the people brought "much more than enough... so Moses gave a commandment... and the people were restrained from bringing, for the material they had was sufficient for all the work to be done-indeed too much." That seldom happens in the American church.

God desires to dwell with man. Let us consider Solomon's temple. David began as a shepherd boy, and at his death gave approximately one hundred million to build the temple. Every detail of the temple was exact. Solomon's temple was majestic. The elders of the church gave one hundred twenty-five million to build the temple plus one hundred million that came from King David. (1 Chronicles 29:6-7)

Consider God's provision for you because your body is the temple of the Holy Spirit. 1 Corinthians 3:16-17 asks, "Do you not know that you are the temple of God and *that* the Spirit of God dwells in you? If anyone defiles the temple of God, God will destroy him. For the temple of God is Holy." Your body is the dwelling place of the Holy Spirit.

God wants to bless you with an abundance that would stagger your mind if you have the faith to practice God's principles of health and prosperity. Remember, you must GIVE your way to wealth.

Many people do not get a blessing because they did not thank God for the last one.

"In everything give thanks; for this is the will of God in Christ Jesus for you." (I Thessalonians 5:18)

Romans 1:21 shows that the refusal to be thankful brings God's judgment. They were not thankful, God gave them over to a reprobate mind. They believed a lie and were damned.

Are you thankful? Thanksgiving is caught, not taught. Thanksgiving is not an emotion; it is a decision, an act of your will. Thanksgiving begins with Thanks-living. Life is God's gift to you; what you do with that life is your gift to God.

Thank God for your talents by accepting them as obligations to be invested in the Kingdom of God. Use your opportunities as a challenge to achieve the impossible. Thank God for each new day and live it as if it were your last one.

You will discover that the spirit of Thanksgiving is the key to releasing the supernatural power of God, that your prayers may be answered, and that supernatural provisions will explode in your life. Thanksgiving is a direct command from God to every Believer, "Be thankful unto Him and bless His name."

Colossians 3:15-17 says, "And let the peace of God rule in your hearts... and be thankful... and whatever you do in word or deed, *do* all in the name of the Lord Jesus, giving thanks to God the Father through Him."

God is too loving to be unkind and too wise to make a mistake. When you are not giving thanks to God, you are in open rebellion against God. Do you complain? What you do not have, is to fault God's provision. Where you are in life, is to fault God's leadership. Who you are, is to fault the sovereignty of God.

Why doesn't God give you more? If you are not thankful for what you have, you will not be given more. The spirit of Thanksgiving is a decision. The spirit of Thanksgiving reflects the presence of the Holy Spirit in you. Ephesians 5:19-20 says, "Speaking to one another in psalms and hymns and spiritual songs, singing and making melody in your heart to the Lord, giving thanks always for all things to God the Father in the name of our Lord Jesus Christ." Spirit-filled people are thankful people.

The spirit of Thanksgiving is necessary to make other forms of prayer effective. Philippians 4:6 tells us to, "Be anxious for nothing, but in everything by prayer and supplication, with thanksgiving, let your requests be made known to God." Start your prayer time with Thanksgiving, not a series of bellyaches. Thanksgiving is the key to releasing God's supernatural power in your life.

Investing in the Kingdom of God is the only financially sure thing on planet Earth.

"As long as he sought the LORD, God made him to prosper." (2 Chronicles 26:5)

A greater financial genius than John Rockefeller asks you to invest in His Kingdom. He will give you a thirty, sixty, one hundred fold harvest. Every offering is an opportunity for you to increase your income.

Money is a great servant, but a terrible master.

In Luke 12:15, Jesus said, "Take heed and beware of covetousness, for one's life does not consist in the abundance of the things he possesses."

Do you own your house, or does your house own you? Do you own your car, or does your car own you? Do not let your possessions take control of your life.

If you have not received anything, it is because you have not given anything.

Proverbs 22:9 says, "He who has a generous eye will be blessed, for he gives of his bread to the poor." The Bible says to give, and it will be given unto you. What have you given?

Blessing Israel brings great prosperity!

The future of the world will be determined by what happens in Jerusalem. Jerusalem holds the key to world peace. "Pray for the peace of Jerusalem: May they prosper who love you." (Psalm 122:6) Jerusalem holds the key to your prosperity.

Through Hagee Ministries, Christians are joining forces with the Jewish people to rescue Jews from all around the world who wish to relocate to Israel. To date, Hagee Ministries has donated more than $100 million to Israeli humanitarian causes. We have done this with the generous help of our partners throughout the world.

Anti-Semitic political groups are on the rise, joining with antidemocratic forces in urging a return to a more closed society. Now with the world in chaos, the environment is more hostile toward Jews than ever, and they are in clear and present danger.

As Christians, we must recognize the critical importance of the Jewish people in God's plan for us all. We must, in direct fulfillment of Jeremiah's prophecy, help bring God's people home to Israel.

Will you help us do more?

NOTES

NOTES

NOTES

NOTES

NOTES

OUR MISSION

Hagee Ministries' mission is to take All the Gospel to All the World
and to share the light and love of Jesus Christ with those that have
traded the truth for shades of grey. Together with our partners,
HM is spreading the bold truth of God's Word across the nations of
the world, not only through our television and radio broadcasts but
through various humanitarian projects, relief efforts, community service
initiatives and worldwide Gospel rallies.

Our partnership makes a real difference in the lives of so many. We receive
thousands of testimonies of God's supernatural provision every day as
a result of hearing His Word through Hagee Ministries. People who live
in nations we may never visit are being changed by receiving the Gospel
through one of our various outreaches. Now, through the internet, we can
even reach households in countries that don't allow the preaching of the
message of Christ.

OUR COMMITMENT

Hagee Ministries
is committed
to God and His
Great Commission,
to win the lost
to Christ, to take
America and the
world back to the
God of our fathers and
continually pray for our
Partners.

*Pastor John
& Diana Hagee*

*Pastor Matt &
Kendal Hagee*

FACEBOOK:
Hagee Ministries
Matt & Kendal Hagee
Cornerstone Church

TWITTER:
@PastorJohnHagee
@PastorMattHagee
@KendalHagee
@HageeMinistries
@saCornerstone

INSTAGRAM:
@PastorJohnHagee
@DianaHagee
@MattHagee
@KendalHagee
@HageeMinistries
@saCornerstone